W9-DCJ-374

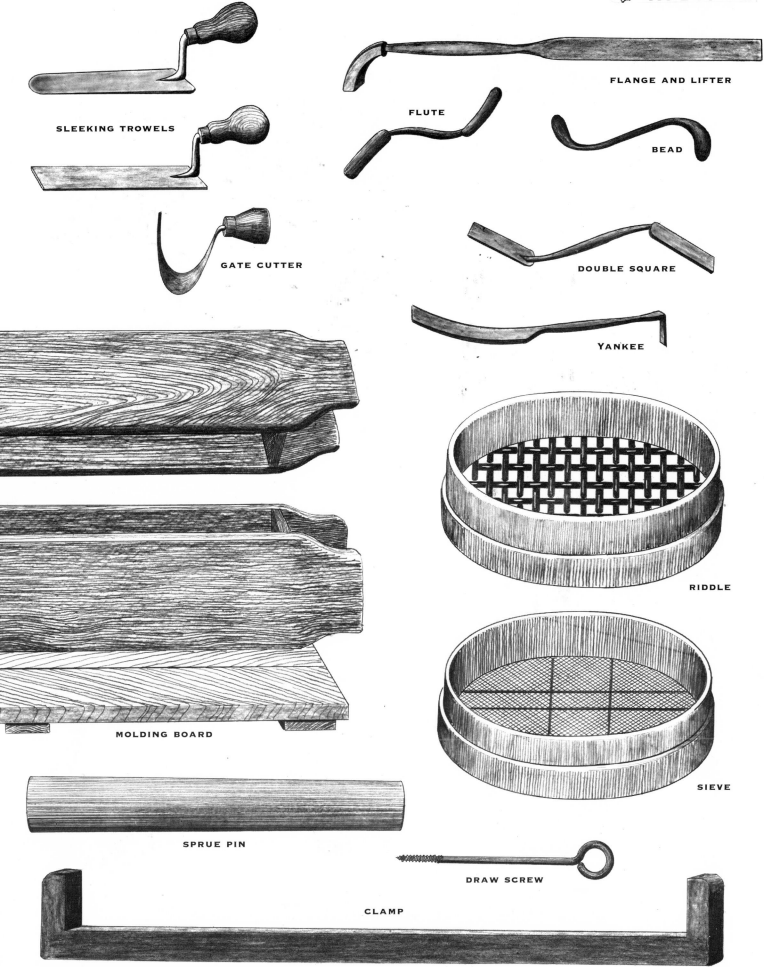

SLEEKING TROWELS

GATE CUTTER

FLUTE

FLANGE AND LIFTER

BEAD

DOUBLE SQUARE

YANKEE

MOLDING BOARD

RIDDLE

SIEVE

SPRUE PIN

DRAW SCREW

CLAMP

Please return to
MRS. RAPPE.

Pouring Iron

A FOUNDRY GHOST STORY

For Wendell, Ernie, Carl, Ed, Mimi, and Russ.
And for Robert Vogel.

POURING IRON

A FOUNDRY GHOST STORY

DAVID WEITZMAN

HOUGHTON MIFFLIN COMPANY
BOSTON 1998

Half an hour from the city of Sacramento, the road climbs up into the Sierra foothills, past old mining towns with names like El Dorado, Rough and Ready, Copperopolis, Fiddletown, Quartz, Chinese Camp, Pioneer, and Gold Run.

Long ago this paved road was no more than two dusty ruts. It was the time of the California Gold Rush, when prospectors headed up into the mountains, their wagons full of provisions and their heads filled with dreams of becoming as rich as kings. A time

when riders galloped down the hill, their saddlebags filled with gold nuggets, headed for the assay offices in Hangtown. A time when half the country, it seemed, was standing waist-deep in the creeks and rivers, panning for gold.

You can still feel the spirit of those days in the Sierra towns. That's why Howard likes to visit his grandparents in the big house overlooking the town of Sutter Creek. The house was built by his great-great-great-grandpa, who came from Wales in the 1870s to work a mile underground in the gold mines.

Many of the buildings here date back to those days, including the old workplace on Eureka Street. Whenever Howard walks by, he peers through the grimy windows. All he can make out are shapes in every shade of dusty gray. A sign hanging above one of the big doors reads *The Knight Foundry.*

This morning, though, the doors are open wide enough for a peek inside. No sooner does he put his eye to the crack than one of the heavy doors rumbles open.

"Hi there! I'm Russ," a man greets him. "You're welcome to come in and look around, if you like. I'm working by myself today, getting ready for the big pour tomorrow."

"By yourself?" Howard asks, unable to take his eyes off the men he sees looking up from their work. Russ follows the boy's gaze into the empty grayness, then looks at Howard with a knowing grin. The foundry is still except for the dust motes dancing in the shafts of sunlight slanting down from the clerestory windows.

In the silence Howard hears the *tink, tink, tink* of metal striking metal. He follows the sound to a man bending quietly over his work. "My name is Wendell, but the guys call me Cast Iron Boitano. I came to work here when I was about your age," Wendell says and then falls silent again, intent on lifting a wooden pattern from the sand. Howard holds his breath as the molder, with a deft motion, draws the pattern clear of the edges of the mold.

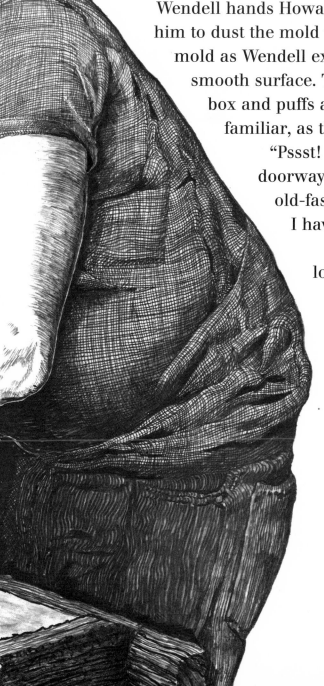

Wendell tells Howard about the first time he lifted a pattern from a mold, when he was an apprentice. "Plump! Sand and pattern fell to my feet in a jumble. Laughter, applause, and cheering exploded through the foundry, and everyone came to see. I didn't know whether to laugh or cry. But my dad brought me a bottle of soda pop and, with mock seriousness, gave a little speech, shook my hand, and welcomed me to the brotherhood of molders."

"You've been doing this a long time," Howard says. "I can tell."

"Sixty years and then some. Just came to work with my dad one day and I've been here ever since. He taught me everything I know about the foundry, my dad did. I was just a kid then, like you. Didn't know nothin' about work. Right out of school. But here's somethin' I'll bet you can do."

Wendell hands Howard a little bag filled with charcoal dust and tells him to dust the mold with it. Howard shakes the bag over the sandy mold as Wendell explains that this fine dust gives the casting a smooth surface. Then Howard reaches for the bellows in the toolbox and puffs away the excess dust. The action feels strangely familiar, as though he's done it a hundred times before.

"Pssst! Pssst! You there!" Howard looks over toward a doorway and sees a man with a gray beard wearing an old-fashioned derby hat. "Yes, you, young man. Come, I have something I'd like to show you."

Howard heads for the dim doorway without looking back.

"I thought you might like to see my invention," the man says. "My name is Samuel Knight, and this is my patented water wheel." Mr. Knight squints at Howard and asks his age. "Fourteen. Well, well. It's too long ago to remember—back in eighteen and fifty-two—but that's the age I was when I began to apprentice as a ship's carpenter, back in Maine it was." Mr. Knight swings his cane about smartly, pointing here and there. "I built this foundry and machine shop to manufacture water wheels—that was back in eighteen and seventy-three—biggest, best-equipped shop in California it was, outside San Francisco.

"There's one of my water motors over there powering the machine shop. Another's running the blowers that force air into the furnace – the blast, we call it. There's another in the pattern shop powering the woodworking tools. Everything in the place is run by water power.

"You'll find Knight water motors running the hoists that lower and lift the miners and the ore at hundreds of gold and copper mines all over the world. Before that the hoists were powered by steam engines. That was an expensive proposition, I'll tell you! Why, the mines were burning ten cords of wood a day. At six dollars a cord, well, you can see how fast that adds up."

Mr. Knight explains how the water – snow-melt collected in a lake high up in the Sierras – plunges down hundreds of feet through big iron pipes ("We make those here, too"). Howard jumps as water explodes out of the nozzle and strikes the buckets on the wheel, sending them spinning in a blur.

"The wheel can be reversed just by pulling or pushing on a lever," Mr. Knight shouts over the splashing and whirring. "Over the years I've been experimenting to find just the right shape for the nozzle and the buckets on the wheel, don't you know, to make them more efficient. Well, that's the gist of it. I've kept you away from your work long enough, young man." Mr. Knight disappears into the shadows, jauntily swinging his cane.

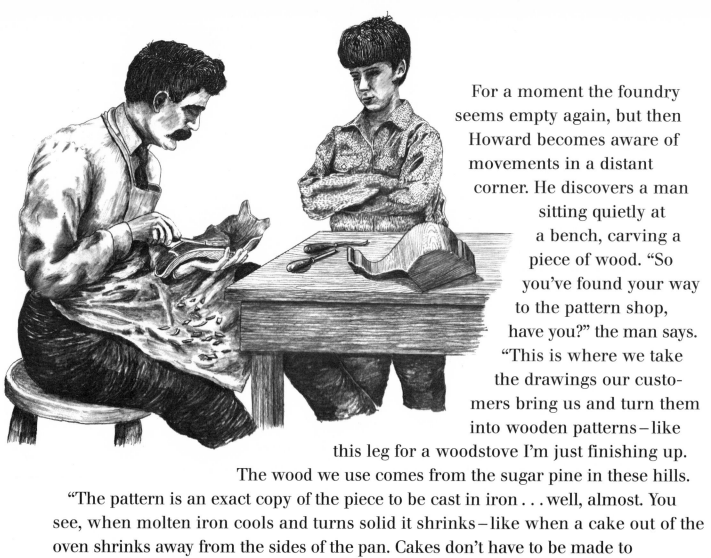

For a moment the foundry seems empty again, but then Howard becomes aware of movements in a distant corner. He discovers a man sitting quietly at a bench, carving a piece of wood. "So you've found your way to the pattern shop, have you?" the man says. "This is where we take the drawings our customers bring us and turn them into wooden patterns—like this leg for a woodstove I'm just finishing up. The wood we use comes from the sugar pine in these hills.

"The pattern is an exact copy of the piece to be cast in iron . . . well, almost. You see, when molten iron cools and turns solid it shrinks—like when a cake out of the oven shrinks away from the sides of the pan. Cakes don't have to be made to exact dimensions, but machine parts do. So, to make up for shrinkage, I make the pattern a little bigger than the finished piece wants to be.

"I also give the sides of the pattern some taper so that the part deepest in the sand is a bit smaller than the top. You'd hardly notice the difference, but when the molder draws the pattern from the sand, this sure makes it easier."

Howard returns to the molding floor and looks over the wooden patterns. They seem eerily familiar. He can't resist the urge to try a mold of his own, and he decides on the pattern for a kind of axle. He feels sure he knows how to do it.

First he sets a molding board in the sand-covered floor, wriggling it around to make sure it is level. Then he places an open wooden box called the drag on the board. Into this he carefully centers one half of the bright red pattern. That done, he turns to the heap of sand, picks up a handful, and squeezes it.

There is more to sand than meets the eye. Each grain is angular, with many points and edges. These angles lock up with other grains to give the sand its strength. Foundrymen call this "sharp" sand. But as the sand is burned by the molten iron, the angles wear off and the grains become rounded and smooth. Dull sand makes a weak mold that will not hold its shape. To make sand even stronger, some clay and water are mixed in.

The molder can tell from the way the sand sticks together in his hand whether it is too moist, too dry, or just right—"tempered," he would say. He knows this in the same way that one can tell whether sand at the beach will form a good sandcastle.

To make the surface of the iron casting smooth, the first sand to go into the mold—the sand that touches the pattern—is clean, sharp sand sifted through a fine sieve.

Howard packs two to three inches of this facing sand all around the pattern with his hands and then shovels in just enough extra sand to cover the pattern five or six inches deep.

Then he rams the sand down around the pattern and against the sides of the drag with the pointed, or peen, end of the rammer. Howard works carefully. If the sand is not rammed up evenly and firmly, the mold may fall apart when the pattern is removed, or the heavy molten iron may ruin the casting. If the sand is rammed up too hard, gases and steam from the hot iron may cause the mold to explode. The skill of ramming up a mold is learned through experience. It's all in the hands, how the rammer feels compressing the sand. And all experience includes a few failures.

When the drag is filled, Howard packs it down with the butt end of the rammer. He strikes off the extra sand so that it is level with the top edge of the drag. Then he pokes holes deep into the sand with a long piece of wire— careful not to hit the pattern— making vents that will help gases and steam escape.

Howard lays another board on the drag, slides it around until it feels solid, and puts on four C-shaped iron clamps. He hammers wooden wedges under the ends of the clamps to hold the two boards tightly to the drag. Howard tries to lift it—ugh!—it won't budge. He tries again, every muscle straining.

"Here, I'll help ya with that." Suddenly the drag comes up. Howard turns to see a man in a tattered old hat. They get the drag up on its side. "That's good. Now let's just ease 'er over onto the bottom board. There you are. It's not hard when there are two of us. Just call out any time you need help. I'm Dave." Before Howard can thank him, the foundryman is gone. Howard stares into the grayness and then turns back to his work, smiling and shaking his head.

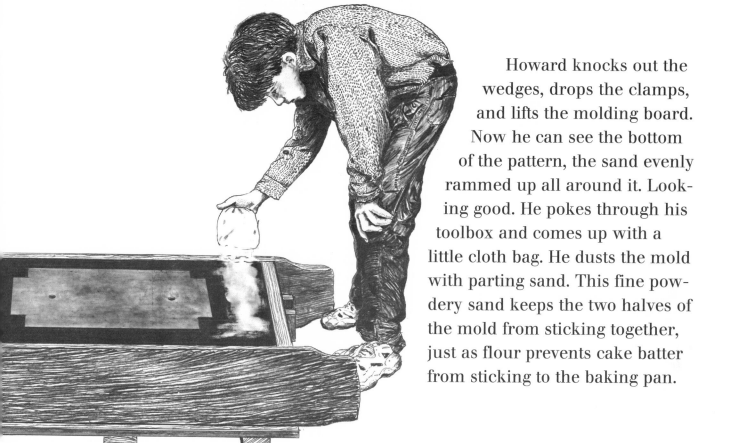

Howard knocks out the wedges, drops the clamps, and lifts the molding board. Now he can see the bottom of the pattern, the sand evenly rammed up all around it. Looking good. He pokes through his toolbox and comes up with a little cloth bag. He dusts the mold with parting sand. This fine powdery sand keeps the two halves of the mold from sticking together, just as flour prevents cake batter from sticking to the baking pan.

Now Howard must add the second half of the pattern, completing the shape of the axle. The two wooden pins on this half of the pattern fit into the two holes drilled on the other half. Like puzzle pieces, the pins hold the two halves of the pattern together and aligned while the molder rams up the cope—the top part of the mold.

"One more time!" Howard feels a bit foolish calling out into the empty foundry, but, sure enough, Dave returns to help him. Together they lift the cope and place it on the drag, careful to engage the wooden pegs that lock the two halves together.

Howard pushes long wooden pins into the sand on both sides of the pattern. Later, when the pins are removed, they leave two openings. One is the sprue, through which the molten iron is poured into the mold. The other is the riser, which allows the air and hot gases to escape. Howard fills the cope as he did the drag, first with facing sand and then with heap sand.

Now Howard faces the moment of truth, a test of just how well he's rammed up his mold. It's time to lift the cope off the drag so that he can remove the pattern. Dave appears and together they lift the cope. Howard's mold holds together.

Howard screws a rod into a hole in the back of the pattern as he has seen Wendell do. He raps on it gently, left and right, front and back. The rapping frees the pattern from the sand. Then he unscrews the rod and replaces it with two draw screws.

"Good work, kid," Dave says, pointing out the fine points of the mold. "Well, I guess we've taught you all we know. You're on your own now." With that he touches his hand to the brim of his hat, a big smile spreading under his bushy mustache, and turns away.

"Wait! Wait a minute," Howard calls out, but the foundryman has already slipped away.

Howard faces the scariest part of completing the mold. He finds inside himself years of confidence and skill—from where he does not know. He grasps the draw screws with both hands, takes a deep breath, and—here goes—carefully draws the pattern straight up out of the sand without touching the sides of the mold. That's one half; one more to go.

He cuts a gate from the open mold to the sprue hole. Then he cuts another gate to the riser. During the pour, molten iron flows down the sprue and through the gate into the mold. The iron fills the mold, then flows out the other gate and up into the riser. This extra iron in the riser also feeds molten metal back into the casting as it shrinks.

Returning from his paperwork in the foundry office, Russ finds Howard working intently over a finished mold. Stopping abruptly, he watches with fascination. After blowing the loose sand out of the mold, Howard attaches a blow pot to the bellows and sprays molasses water. The sticky sprinkling will harden into a smooth, tough surface ready to receive the iron.

"Hey, Russ," Howard says to the ironmaster, "I know this sounds weird, but have you ever seen . . . uh . . . ghosts in the foundry?"

Russ smiles. "Yeah. Sometimes, when I'm here alone, I'll glimpse something out of the corner of my eye, someone moving about in the shadows. But when I look up, no one's there. I just figure those old guys who used to work here, you know, if they loved the work as much as we do, they must come back from time to time. Yeah, kid, I've seen them."

Together they close up the completed mold and walk out into the long shadows of early evening. Russ puts his shoulder to the big doors and slides them closed, snaps the padlock, and invites Howard to have an ice cream cone at the drugstore soda fountain. The foundry is still except for the swallows swooping in and out of the windows high above.

The next morning Howard returns to find the foundry transformed. The stillness has given way to the noisy flurry of a pour day.

And it's hot. Tons of coke – coal roasted until only pure carbon remains – glow in the foundry furnace, awaiting the first iron charge. Early this morning, Russ covered the cupola bottom with a floor of sand, lit a pile of kindling, and got a good fire going with cordwood before throwing in the first shovelfuls of coke. Then he lit small wood fires in each of the ladles to harden and dry the clay coating inside.

Carl, the foundry owner, is here too. Like the owners before him, going back to Sam Knight, Carl does whatever needs to be done—marketing, sales, pattern-making, molding, tending the cupola, helping with the pour, machining finished pieces, even delivering them in his pickup truck.

"Watch your face!" The warning that the blast is about to be turned on echoes through the foundry. *WHOMP! Whoosh!* With a great puff of smoke and flame, air is forced up through the hot coke, turning it from red to flaming orange and yellow.

Now the pace picks up. Russ races up the ramp leading from the molding floor to the charging deck. Around him, arranged in charges of 750 pounds each, are piles of scrap iron—engine blocks, stoves, man-hole covers, grates, pipes, truck parts—all broken up into chunks. After putting in the first charge of iron, Russ counts out shovelfuls of limestone—crushed rock that helps the iron flow through the flaming mass of coke. He runs down the ramp again, this time to seal the tapping hole with a bod, a red clay plug. In a few minutes, molten iron will begin pooling at the bottom of the cupola.

At timed intervals, the cupola man
and his helpers will put in layers of coke,
layers of limestone, and charges of iron
until the pour is finished. Russ might add
chunks of steel to the last iron charge
for special castings that must be very hard
and durable.

The blast has brought the temperature
inside the cupola up to 2,500 degrees.
Russ has no thermometers to tell
him how hot it is, but, like gen-
erations of ironmasters before

him, he can tell from the color of the coke and the consistency of the iron. He motions Howard to look into one of the mica lenses in the tuyères—the pipes that carry the blast into the fiery heart of the furnace.

"It's raining," Russ calls out when the iron has begun to trickle down through the coke. "Pour will be at eleven-thirty... *two*," he declaims with the seriousness of an orator.

"Let's go to lunch."

"Iron's up!" Russ announces from the foundry doorway. One by one the crew straggles in, still logy from lunch and a sun-warmed nap on the grassy banks of the creek. Talk has been of the weekend, fishing, panning for gold, favorite swimming holes, and the coming World Series. And they watched a cinnamon teal and her ducklings swimming in the quiet water that runs down from the snowy mountains.

"Let's go," comes Russ's insistent call. "Tap it." Each man picks up his tool and takes his place in front of the cupola and the waiting ladle. Howard picks up a skimmer. Russ begins chipping away at the clay bod until yellow-orange iron, first a trickle and then a torrent, streams down the spout into the ladle.

Suddenly, amidst the smoke and showers of sparks, the ghostly figures of Wendell and Dave appear to take up their old places. Wendell stands waiting, poised to plug the tap hole as soon as the ladle is full. He lunges forward, firmly setting the bod and stemming the flow of iron. Dave reaches into the ladle with a hooked skimmer and removes a popping, sparking glob of slag that has floated to the top. Wendell and Dave grasp the handles of the ladle shank and, signaling to Ed at the crane, set a graceful dance in motion.

In Wendell's and Dave's practiced hands the ladle glides up and away from the cupola toward a huge mold. The iron must not be allowed to cool. Swiftly but carefully, Wendell positions the beak and tips the ladle until yellow metal pours down into the sprue. Howard uses the hook of his skimmer to hold a glob of slag back, the hot metal singeing his face. Molten iron appears in the riser just as the last drops leave the lip of the ladle. A thousand pounds of iron in a single pour. Just right. "Let's go home," Wendell calls out. That's Ed's cue to swing the empty ladle back to the cupola.

The pour goes on through the afternoon hours without a pause—three more granary scale weights, columns for a cast-iron storefront, machine parts, a water turbine wheel, brake shoes for an old locomotive, gears, pulleys, Howard's axle, and dozens of other items. By the time they finish, the sun has dropped below the hills, leaving the casting floor in dark shadow. As the crew puts away the tools and cleans up, Russ makes an entry in his journal:

Friday, August 25, 1997. Total gray iron: 5,750. Perfect to the pound.
No runouts. Mom duck showed off her new ducklings on the creek today.
Lots of trout. Looks like a good weekend for fishing.

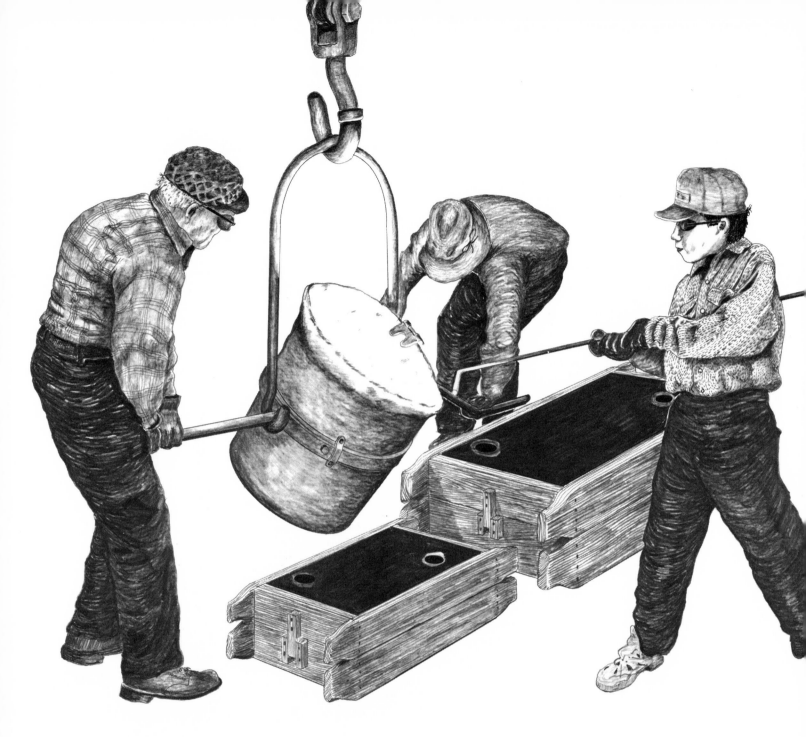

Howard returns to the foundry Monday morning with some sadness. He has come early so he can be alone for a while. In an hour he'll have to say goodbye to Grandma and Grandpa and leave his new friends, Sutter Creek, and the gold country to go home.

The castings have been cooling all weekend. In place of the orderly rows of molds are black sand heaps and gray iron castings. "You boys are still doing good work," comes a voice breaking the silence. "Keeping the foundryman's craft alive, you are."

An elderly man ambles across the floor. "And which casting did you mold, son?" Howard finds his axle and displays it proudly, searching the warm, wrinkled face that looks so familiar. "Well, now," the man says, rubbing his fingers appreciatively over the casting, "that's solid workmanship, all right. You know, I've seen a lot of castings on this floor, molded thousands of them myself. You've done a good piece of work here, young man."

"Do you work here?"

The man laughs and looks around wistfully. "Oh, yes . . . well, what I mean to say is, I did work here. Started here when I was just a kid, about your age. Learned foundry work from Mr. Sam Knight himself, I did. Back then there were more than forty men working here, sometimes nights as well as days. Yep . . . yep. But that was a long, long time ago." He rubs his eyes quickly with his sleeve. "I worked here for more than forty years, twenty of them with my son, Wendell, right where we stand. Yep, forty years. Seems like yesterday."

The big door rumbles open, splashing white sunlight across the foundry floor. Howard turns to the old man, but he has disappeared. The hulking figure of Russ strides over and kneels in the sand. He examines the boy's casting. "Hmm . . . the sprue and riser are just right," he says, almost to himself. "Not a bit of scab—as smooth a surface as I've ever seen. Well done. Outstanding!" He looks at Howard and then at the casting, stroking his bearded chin, mumbling "hmm" over and over. And then he gestures to Howard with a raised finger to wait there a minute.

When the ironmaster returns from the foundry office, he holds an old, faded photograph. "I found this while I was going through the files this weekend. And I noticed something. Something kind of unusual, even strange, you might say. This picture must have been taken, oh, around 1902, because Wendell's dad looks to be about fourteen years old. But look here. See the kid on the right? Is it my imagination or what, Howard? He looks just like you."

HISTORIC KNIGHT FOUNDRY TODAY

You can visit the Knight Foundry down at the end of Eureka Street in Sutter Creek, California. There you'll see one of America's earliest foundry machine shops, one of the few still powered by water.

Since it first opened in 1873, Knight & Co. has manufactured hundreds of water wheels. In 1897 they made fifty-eight-inch-diameter bronze wheels for a hydroelectric plant in Ogden, Utah, the largest in the country, which electrified Salt Lake City.

Knight also manufactured mining equipment to accommodate the rush to extract gold from the ore-rich hills—stamp mills, hoist works, ore cars, rock crushers, centrifugal pumps, and immense dredger buckets weighing 14,000 pounds that were used to deepen the harbors at San Francisco, Tacoma, and Seattle.

Among historic Knight Foundry's recent products are parts for mining, lumbering, and agricultural machinery. The foundry has been involved in historic preservation, making everything from replacement parts for steam locomotives and antique automobiles to reproductions of architectural iron work for the California state capitol.

The Knight Foundry is listed on the National Register of Historic Places and has been honored by the American Society of Mechanical Engineers as a National Historic Mechanical Engineering Landmark.

Copyright © 1998 by David Weitzman

Photographs courtesy of the Knight Foundry and the Amador County Archives

All rights reserved. For information about permission to reproduce selections from this book, write to Permissions, Houghton Mifflin Company, 215 Park Avenue South, New York, New York 10003.

The text of this book is set in Walbaum.
The illustrations are pencil, and pen and ink.

Library of Congress Cataloging-in-Publication Data

Weitzman, David L.
Pouring iron / David Weitzman.
p. cm.
Summary: While visiting his grandparents in Sutter Creek, California, Howard goes to the historic Knight Foundry and experiences firsthand the process of creating all sorts of cast iron products.
ISBN 0-395-84170-4
1. Knight Foundry–Juvenile fiction. [1. Knight Foundry–Fiction.
2. Iron founding–Fiction. 3. Sutter Creek (Calif.)–Fiction. 4. California–Fiction.] I. Title.
PZ7.W448184Po 1998
[Fic]–dc21 97-49085 CIP AC

Manufactured in the United States of America
HOR 10 9 8 7 6 5 4 3 2 1

.ase return to
MRS. RAPPE.

BUTT

DOUBLE ENDER

BELLOWS

YANKEE

GATE CUTTER

FLAT,
D-HANDLE
SHOVEL

COPE

FLOOR RAMMER

DRAG
(OR NOWEL)

BLOW POT

HAND RAMMERS

SWAB

PEEN